CHOSEN WITH ESTHER

20 Devotionals to Awaken Your Calling, Guide Your Heart, and Empower You To Lead By God's Design

David Ramos

Thank You!

I appreciate you taking the time to check out my book. As a thank you, I would like to send you the gift *Dreaming with Joseph: 12 Devotionals to Inspire Your Faith, Encourage Your Heart, and Help Your Realize God's Plan.*

To claim your FREE copy simply go to RamosAuthor.com and enter your email address.

.

Table of Contents

Introduction

I did not know what it felt like to be chosen growing up. I was a husky kid (that's the nice way of saying I was overweight). I wore glasses, braces, and needed speech therapy. It's not difficult to imagine why I was picked last, picked on, and dateless.

My situation began to change in my early college years. That is when I dove into the Scriptures and began to realize something important: how God saw me. I read stories of these amazing characters, the adventurous lives they led, and I wanted that for me. If God could use imperfect people to shape history, maybe He could use me for something great as well.

Esther was also used to not being picked. Except for her kind, older cousin Mordecai, she was alone in a strange land. Esther had no idea what God had planned for her, because she did not yet see herself as He did.

God chose Esther because He saw who Esther truly was. He saw her potential, her character, and her strength. He knew the trials that were going to come for the Jewish people, and He chose to put her right in the middle of it all.

God has done the same with you. He looked into the depths of your heart, and into the furthest reaches of your abilities and said "I have made you for this." This trial is not a coincidence and this moment is not a mistake. You are here for a reason, and I believe the book of Esther will help you see that.

Over the next 20 days, you will be guided through the story of this brave queen. You will see God's hand guiding events, even as He appears to be silent. And you will be introduced to the absolute worst and best humankind has to offer.

I pray you will be stirred towards your calling, motivated by your worth, and convinced that you too have been chosen with Esther...

The Danger of Excess

Day 1

Esther 1:1-9

The story of Esther begins in the royal halls of the Persian king, Xerxes. It is difficult to know exactly which ruler the story is referring to, since the names of kings were shared down through generations. But it is within the realm of possibility that this Xerxes is the Xerxes.

A little history lesson will help you see why he is so important. Xerxes was the grandson of Cyrus the Great. Cyrus was the ruler who allowed the Jewish people to return home after the Babylonians had captured them and destroyed Jerusalem (the books of Daniel, Jeremiah, Ezekiel, and Isaiah all talk about this terrible time). Because Cyrus allowed the Jewish people to return home, many Jews supported the Persian empire and even stayed behind to continue living in foreign lands.

All that is to say, people liked Xerxes. His family had been friendly to the Jews, and there was no reason to think he wouldn't continue that trend. But still,

Xerxes was no pushover. If you have ever heard of the story of the 300 Spartans, this was the king they were fighting against. In an age where someone could conquer a continent with twenty thousand men in their army – Persia could amass a force of nearly half a million soldiers. [i]

Xerxes and the Persians knew no limits, and that shows through in this opening scene. The beginning of Esther records an excessive, almost ridiculous, banquet. Xerxes has invited leaders from across the land to view his wealth and party for over six months. The attendees were surrounded by gold, jewels, and endless wine. There were no restrictions, and as we will soon see, no safeguards against senseless actions.

Off to the side, there is a second banquet run by Xerxes' queen: Vashti. Whereas Xerxes's banquet takes a paragraph to describe, Vashti's is summarized in a single sentence. The narrator uses this to help us see how different the king and queen truly are. It is this difference which will incite the coming events.

Esther is a story of risk and redemption. But it is also a story of restraint.

On one side, we will see characters with no limits who do what they want, when they want, regardless of the consequences. On the other, we will watch characters who move from a place of wisdom rather than from a place of fear or anger.

We always have a choice on how we will act in a certain situation. What the majority does, is not what we have to do. Sometimes, standing out from the crowd can ruin your life, but other times it can save it.

Takeaway: Excess, in any area of life, will eventually lead to pain.

Prayer: Heavenly Father, You have given me this one life. Please help me live with wisdom, moderation, and boldness.

David Ramos

A Better Observer

Day 2
Esther 1:10-22

The banquet scene escalates as King Xerxes summons his wife, Vashti, into the hall so that he could show her off. Vashti refuses, and for good reason. This type of showing off was for concubines or prostitutes – not for women of honor, and certainly not for a queen.

Xerxes is infuriated. He gathers noblemen and lawmakers to decide what to do. The commentator, Frederic Bush, words it perfectly: "not knowing how to handle his recalcitrant wife, the king turns the affair into a matter of state."[ii] Rather than respecting his wife enough to talk with her, he transforms an incident based on pride into a full-fledged crisis of the kingdom.

The king and his men decide to issue an edict, or an official order, that women must respect their husbands. Along with this, Vashti is banished from the king's presence.

Why did all this have to happen, and how does it lead to the story of Esther? As we will see, Vashti's role as queen needed to be fulfilled by someone. But aside from that, this scene plays the important role of setting the tone and temper for the rest of the story.[iii] It's important to understand the *type* of story Esther is. While most of our modern retellings characterize Esther as a drama, the truth is that Esther is much closer to what the ancient world called comedy.

When we think of comedy we think of silliness, laughter and satire. But there are also other elements present that we don't always pay attention to like irony, reversal and exaggeration.[iv] Esther is not a light, funny story; but it is an ironic one. The book of Esther wants us to realize how ridiculous the Persians are. It wants us to feel fear and anger when the bad guys are ahead, and hopeful that a reversal will make the world right again.

Esther is an emotional and complicated story that requires us not only to understand what is happening, but how it is being communicated.

This method of study can also help us become better Christians. When we take events at face value or react to circumstances without diving a little deeper, we usually miss what God may be trying to teach us. Xerxes did not take the time to understand why his wife did not want to come. All he could think about what that she disrespected him when in fact, he was the one disrespecting her. In the same way, careful study of our lives will often lead to drastically different, and better, results.

Takeaway: As we observe what is happening in our lives, it's important that we also learn to ask the why and how behind it.

Prayer: Lord, teach me to be a person of depth. Even though I will never understand everything, guide me to be patient and attentive in every situation.

David Ramos

Truth And Potential

Day 3

Esther 2:1-4

After the whirlwind of activity in Chapter 1, Chapter 2 begins on a more solemn note.

The king's "*fury had subsided*" and now we can see the recognizable look of regret on his face. Only now does he realize the consequences of his drunken actions. Vashti is gone. His queen has been banished and it is all his fault.

His attendants quickly offer a solution, before his sorrow turns into anger against them. They want to help him find a new wife. The servants lay out the entire plan before the king in detail, and he agrees.

One thing which stands out to me as I read about King Xerxes, and that will become more apparent throughout the story, is how quick he is to take other people's advice. Of course, a king hires counselors to help him make better decisions. But that isn't quite what is happening here. The king has surrounded himself with attendants who only want to make the king happy; to the detriment of giving him sound, wise advice.

The king is, in simplest terms, spoiled. And there is no one brave enough to tell him otherwise.

In many Biblical stories, there are two main characters readers are presented with. One is the hero. The person who is on God's side, and whose actions we should model our lives after. The other is the rival or enemy. This person makes the wrong choices and ends up paying a very steep price for their actions (*examples*: David and Saul, Moses and Pharaoh).

In most of these stories, we are taught to focus on the hero; to learn what they did and did not do. But that is only half the lesson. Many times, some of the best lessons are hidden in the lives of these rivals.

King Xerxes is one of the rivals in the story of Esther. He does not always make the wrong choice, but he is certainly not someone we would want to model our lives after. The reason Xerxes can be such a dangerous character is because of the situation we touched on above. He has surrounded himself with people who are unwilling to tell him the hard things, the uncomfortable truths. Because of that, he will always act and rule below his potential.

What voices have you surrounded yourself with? Can the people in your life tell you difficult, uncomfortable things? Or have you groomed your relationships to only tell you what you want to hear?

You don't want people around who are always negative or "against you." That is not what I am saying. What I am saying is that it is far too easy to only listen to words that reinforce our beliefs and actions. It's much harder to hear messages that challenge us, push our limits, and call us out on our shortcomings.

I know I have been guilty of this. But if we choose to live like Xerxes, to surround ourselves with only the things we want to hear – just like him, we will always live below the potential God has called us to.

Takeaway: What we allow ourselves to listen to and believe, will profoundly shape our lives.

Prayer: God, You have given us Your word precisely so that it could shape our lives. Help me to listen even when it is difficult.

David Ramos

By Design

The scene shifts away from the king and his minions to two Jews living in the Persian kingdom.

The first is Mordecai. The text gives us a little background on his character. He is from the tribe of Benjamin, specifically a descendant of Kish. This information will play an important role later in the story.

The second person introduced is Mordecai's younger cousin, an orphan he took in as his own, named Hadassah (her Hebrew name), or Esther (her non-Hebrew name). It was common practice for Jews in the Diaspora (those who did not return to Israel after their exile ended) to have a "vernacular" name. This allowed them to fit into their foreign societies better, as well as avoid possible conflicts because of their heritage.[v]

Xerxes' decision to find a new wife has gone into effect, and Esther has been pulled into the running.

She is placed under the care of one of the king's servants, and before long she wins his favor. Esther is beautiful. But more than that, Esther carries herself with a wisdom far beyond her years as we will see.

In the background, during Esther's beginning rise, we see Mordecai checking in on her every day. He has taken the role of adoptive father seriously and the relationship between Esther and Mordecai will play a vital role in the challenges ahead.

The focus of this short section seems to be on the favor Esther finds with everyone she meets. She was both an orphan and a foreigner. Esther did not come from a well-known family, and it certainly does not appear that Mordecai was anywhere near being wealthy. If she had had a choice, Esther likely would have never entered this "beauty contest" in the first place!

There's a powerful but simple truth present in this passage. One we often hear, but rarely believe.

God has already given us everything we need to fulfill the purpose He will call us to.

So many of the events that had to happen to get to this point were never Esther's choice. She did not choose to lose her parents, or be taken in by her older cousin. She never chose to be made beautiful in just the way the king would find most appealing. And yet, when the time came, all of these seemingly disconnected variables came together to move Esther into exactly the place she needed to be so that she could accomplish exactly what God had set for her to do.

Nothing of your story is by accident. The way you look, the way you speak. What happened to you in the past, where you are living now, even the fact that you are reading this book – all of it was by design to get you where you need to be so that you can begin to fulfill the calling God has assigned you to do.

Takeaway: There are no coincidences, only designed opportunities.

Prayer: Heavenly Father, I cannot fathom how You have designed every part of this world, and yet still care about the details of my life. Help me seize the opportunities You guide me towards, and trust that You have already given me what I need.

David Ramos

Unchangeable Value

Day 5
Esther 2:12-18

We are introduced to Xerxes' beauty competition right away. Once again, the theme of excess appears to play a major role.

Before the women can even meet the king, they are given *"beauty treatments"* for a full year. This included perfume, makeup, and, probably, changes to their diet as well. After this lengthy process, each woman would have the opportunity to spend one evening with the king. The writer of Esther does a masterful job of giving the scene a PG rating. However, the text is clear since each woman would go to the king in the evening and not return until morning, they were there to please the king's sexual desires.

In the midst of all this excess (superfluous amounts of time, treatments, and desires), Esther stands out once again. This time for her simplicity. When going in to see the king, the text tells us that *"she asked for nothing."* Even when everything around her said that she needed to have, and be, and do more – she resigned herself to less.

We do not get any words from Esther during the entire first part of the book. But from what is to come, we can guess what she may have been thinking during this process: I am who God has made me to be, and that is enough to fulfill what he has called me to do. It is an echo of yesterday's lesson, and I believe the more we read in Esther's story, the more prevalent it will become.

The king chose Esther to be his queen not because of the certain treatment she underwent or the garment she wore. He chose Esther because she was her own person, and did not try to hide behind tactics and gifts. Either the king would want her for who she was, or he wouldn't.

I heard a story recently that can help us see the lesson in today's passage.

One day a speaker held up a $20 bill in front of his audience and asked, "Who would like this $20 bill?" Hands went up across the room.

He then dropped the bill to the ground and began to trample it under his shoe. After a few moments of this, he picked it back up and asked "Now, who still wants it?" Again, the same hands popped up across the room.

The speaker said, "You have all learned a valuable lesson. No matter what happened to the money, you still wanted it because it did not decrease in value. In the same way, we will be dropped and dirtied by this life. But just like the $20 bill, you will never lose your value."

Esther knew her value. Treatments, perfumes, and gifts did not change her value; neither would it have changed if the king had chosen a different woman. Esther was a daughter of the True King, our Heavenly Father, and that was enough.

You are enough. Regardless of the people that have trampled on you, the disappointments life has thrown at you, or the opportunities that did not choose you. You are valuable. You are loved. Most of all, you are alive which means God still has a plan for your life and a reason for your journey.

Takeaway: Nothing in this life can subtract from the value God has given me.

Prayer: Lord, You have told me that I am fearfully and wonderfully made. Give me the courage to believe that today.

David Ramos

The Work of Grace

Day 6

Esther 2:19-23

Soon after Esther is chosen to be queen, a plot against the king erupts.

The text is brief, so we never know what caused the king's officers to conspire against Xerxes, or what their plan actually was. All we do know is that before they could take any action, Mordecai foils their plan by telling Esther, and having her tell the king.

The king acts immediately and executes the two traitors. Xerxes is indebted to Mordecai. It was common for Persian kings to have celebrations for their "benefactors." [vi] The fact that Mordecai was not rewarded right away should leave us curious. As we will see, this plays a vital role in the events to come.

In the background of this foiled plot, we are reminded that Esther has continued to keep her Jewish identity hidden. Mordecai has helped her get this far, and hopefully his wisdom will continue to keep his cousin safe.

There are a number of ideas present in this short passage: the idea of God's perfect timing, since Mordecai happened to be right where he needed to be in order to save the king; or of the power of humility, since Esther turned over all the credit to Mordecai. But the idea I want to dive deeper into is that of Mordecai's delayed reward.

One of the most popular, modern Christian beliefs is that of reaping and sowing: what you put into something, is ultimately what you get out of it. Now, this is definitely a Biblical principle, since we can find good examples of it all across Scripture (Galatians 6:7, Job 4:8, Matthew 26:52, 2 Corinthians 9:6). But if you think sowing and reaping is the heart of Christianity, you are missing something so much more extraordinary.

You see, the gospel is all about what was undeserved. Humans did not deserve a Savior. Jesus did not deserve to die. Yet this gift, this costly reward, is what has been offered to us freely. We do not have to work for it. There is no sowing and reaping our salvation. There is only grace.

When you read the stories of Esther and Mordecai, and learn about how they saved their people from destruction, please do not think that they earned the right to do so. In reality, it was all God's generous grace.

Grace allowed Mordecai to hear about the conspiracy. Grace is what moved Esther into the position where she could warn the king. And the king's delay in rewarding Mordecai was an act of grace, so that a bigger grace could be shown to all the Jewish people.

God's grace is always at work in our lives, because we could never deserve all He has planned for us.

Takeaway: We can neither earn God's grace, nor imagine where it will take us.

Prayer: Jesus, You shower me with grace every single day. Lead me to live out this undeserved kindness well.

David Ramos

Anger And Authority

Day 7

Esther 3:1-6

The story fast-forwards once again and we are introduced to another major character in the book of Esther, the man who will become known as the enemy of the Jews: Haman.

The first thing we learn about Haman is that he has pleased the king in some way. Enough to have him promoted to *"a seat of honor higher than all the other nobles."* Haman is an important man, and somebody who wants that importance recognized.

It seems that everyone shows Haman the respect he desires except for one person: Mordecai. We are never given specifics as to why Mordecai chose not to kneel or *"pay him honor."* But what we can know is that race played a major part.

You see, Haman is an Agagite. This exact term is not one we find elsewhere in Scripture. However, through some careful study, scholars have found a link. There was a ruler named Agag, king of the Amalekites.[vii] Agag was a vicious enemy of Israel and his battle against King Saul and the prophet Samuel eventually ended in his death. From that time forward, there has been a bitter hatred between the Amalekites and the Israelites (Jews).

Haman's "Agagite" background is likely just another name for his Amalekite heritage. Haman grew up believing that the Jews were his enemies. And now, here was this lone Jewish man standing against him and disrespecting his power. He wouldn't tolerate it. So Haman began to construct a plot. Not just to take revenge against Mordecai, but to destroy all of the Jewish people.

Before we see what comes of Haman's anger, we should ask an important question. Was Mordecai justified in disrespecting Haman?

On the one hand, the Bible has made it clear that we should respect those in power. "Let everyone be subject to the governing authorities, for there is no authority except that which God has established" (Romans 13:1a).

But on the other hand, Scripture is ripe with examples of God's people fighting injustice and evil by going up against the dominant power. Just look at Acts 4, 5, and 12. The disciple, Peter, even ends one of these chapters by saying, "We must obey God rather than men" (Acts 5:29).

This is a difficult subject and one we can hardly begin to dive into in just a short devotion. But the message is deeply applicable for today's world. As Christians, we are called to obey God above anything and anyone else. And Mordecai's example is one we can follow.

He did not argue against Haman or try to get his honor revoked. Instead he quietly, yet powerfully, stood while everyone else bowed and without a word, exposed where his priorities lay.

In this life, there will be times when we will need to reveal whose authority we truly follow. I hope we can do so as gracefully and confidently as Mordecai.

Takeaway: God's authority should be the most important authority in our lives.

Prayer: Dear God, I pray that you will help me live as a good citizen of this world, but also give me the boldness to never forget my true citizenship in Your

Kingdom. And when those two conflict, grant me the wisdom to act.

Haman's Hard Heart

Day 8
Esther 3:7-15

Haman will not let his anger for Mordecai go to rest. He schedules a meeting with the king and, through a series of lies, convinces Xerxes that the allowing the Jewish people to live in his kingdom will eventually lead to its destruction.

Almost immediately, Xerxes acts and sends out a decree saying that on a certain day, eleven months from now, all the people of his kingdom will be allowed to kill their Jewish neighbors and claim the Jewish property as their own. With lightning speed, the edict is sent across the kingdom.

This scene has a chilling end. Verse 15 tells us that while the entire city is afraid and confused by this news, the king and Haman sit together and drink. They display a "callous indifference" that is hard to believe.[viii]

Two important themes run throughout this scene. First, is one we have encountered before: excess.

Instead of Haman seeking revenge upon the man who disrespected him, or even taking revenge upon Mordecai's entire family, Haman opts to destroy an entire people group! There is no sense or logic guiding Haman's decision. Only pure, reckless pride.

The second theme is the irony of how the Persian government works. Do you remember in the first chapter when Vashti refused to honor the king's request? It became a huge ordeal. All levels of government were called in to help Xerxes decide how he should deal with his wife. He treated it with the utmost importance. Now, we see the total opposite. Whereas Xerxes needed dozens of advisors to help him with his wife, he and Haman decided to eradicate an entire population all on their own.

In the Bible, we see the theme of God blinding the eyes and hardening the hearts of his enemies. When Moses was attempting to free his people, the LORD "hardened Pharaoh's heart" (Exodus 9:12). In the New Testament, we see a similar phrase, "[God] has blinded their eyes and hardened their heart, lest they see with their eyes, and understand with their heart, and turn, and I would heal them" (John 12:40).

When we look at Xerxes and Haman's decision, we are actually seeing their blindness and hardened hearts. Xerxes and Haman literally do not know better because they have been made unaware of how horrible their actions truly are. By ignoring who God is and what God wants, they have become separated from what is right in a profound way.

The lesson in these verses is more of a warning. We may think that Xerxes and Haman were deeply evil; when in reality, they had simply been separated from God's truth and goodness for so long that they had lost their understanding of what is right and good. When we ignore God, or trust our own thoughts over His wisdom, that is the beginning of our blindness and hardness.

Every person is capable of terrible actions. But every sinner is also invited to God's cleansing grace.

Takeaway: Ignoring God can lead to blindness. Blindness can lead us down paths we never thought we would go. But God's grace always offers us a way back to Him.

Prayer: I don't always want to do things Your way Lord. Forgive me, and keep my eyes open and my heart soft towards what is pleasing to You.

Knowing God

Day 9

Esther 4:1-3

The author of Esther offers us a more intimate look at the terror the Jews are feeling by showing us Mordecai.

Because of Mordecai's position of power, it's no surprise that he was likely one of the first Jewish persons to hear the news. It's hard to imagine the pain and fear he must be feeling. Everyone he knows, hundreds of families, countless innocent faces – all facing extermination because of an enemy he angered. Mordecai clothes himself in traditional mourning clothes and cries out, desperately.

But all is not lost. Even in this moment of extreme agony, Mordecai somehow holds onto hope. Our commentator, Frederic Bush, writes of Mordecai's cry that it had the connotation of a "plaintive cry, a call for help."[ix]

Even in the darkest of moments, Mordecai refuses

to submit to current circumstances. As we will see, his cry for help may have been heard by just the right person.

How can we learn to hope like Mordecai? To believe that all is not lost, even when everything around us tells us differently?

Many other characters in Scripture have found themselves in similar situations. David against Goliath. Naomi after the death of her family. Abraham on the way to sacrifice his only son. What sustained these characters is what, I believe, sustained Mordecai. And it is also what can sustain us. That thing is knowing God's character.

When we know more of *who* God is, we will learn to trust *what* He does, and doesn't do, as all being for our ultimate good. Even though the text does not tell us about Mordecai's relationship with God, I believe what we see of his own character shows us that Mordecai was a man after God's own heart. He cared for the orphan, was honest in his dealings with others, and cared deeply about the welfare of God's people.

When we learn about God we cannot help but be shaped by our understanding of Him. So often the answer we are seeking from God is simply *"come and know me better."*

Takeaway: Our hope in God is fueled by our knowledge of His character.

Prayer: Gracious God, I will never be able to understand how perfect You are. But I pray that You will give me a glimpse each day, so that I might always trust in You.

Real Threat, False Fear

Day 10
Esther 4:4-11

Mordecai's cry for help has reached Esther's servants and once they tell her about Mordecai, her heart breaks.

At first, Esther tries to mend Mordecai's sadness by sending him clothes. But to no avail. Next, she sends out one of her servants to find out what is really going on; what could possibly have driven her cousin to such actions. The servant returns and explains all that Mordecai had found out.

Mordecai not only told Esther what had happened, he also urged her to *"go into the king's presence."* At this point, we can also feel the fear running through Esther's bones. She has just found out that the lives of her people are at risk. And now, Mordecai has asked her to enter the king's presence. An action, which itself, could mean immediate death.

There is no easy answer here. Esther sends a

message back to Mordecai explaining the situation and, indirectly, pleads for another option.

Fear weighs heavily upon this scene. Mordecai's fear that the Jewish people will be eradicated. Esther's fear for her own life, and that there is nothing she can do to help her people.

I recently took a course on fear, and what the Bible has to say about it. It was incredibly helpful because the Bible truly says much on the subject. However, I want to focus on how the class defined the term fear: "a distressing emotion aroused by impending danger...whether the threat is real or imagined."[x]

Fear is not the thing we are afraid of; it is our reaction to that thing. Fear can be useful because it tells our minds and bodies what could go wrong and why that is a bad thing. But, fear does not always tell the truth. Nor does it present us with all the options.

Fear limits us. It limits what we see. It limits the way we think. It stops us, many times before we have even began. Mordecai and Esther had very real reasons to fear. Their lives really were at risk. But being afraid never has to be the end of your story.

There's a difference between a roadblock and a

dead-end. A roadblock is temporary. It can be repaired, detoured, or just plowed through. A dead-end is exactly what it sounds like: the end of the road. There is no way through a dead-end because there is nothing on the other side.

Fear wants us to believe that situations are dead-ends when they are really just roadblocks. Don't believe your fear. Amazing things can happen when you choose to move through the roadblocks.

Takeaway: Your fear never has to be the end of the road.

Prayer: I do not want my life to be run by fear, Lord. Teach me to cast every one of my fears into Your protective arms.

David Ramos

Stepping Towards Purpose

Day 11
Esther 4:12-17

Esther's fearful response reaches back to Mordecai, and he responds to his cousin with both wisdom and hard truth.

Mordecai urges Esther, *"this horrible thing will reach you too, if you don't do anything then all of us will perish."* But he does not end on a grave note. Instead, with wisdom and tact, he reaches down into the heart of the issue. Deeper than the fear. Deeper than her self-doubt. Mordecai touches upon her desire, our human desire, to have a purpose greater than ourselves. *"Maybe this is why God brought you to the palace...maybe your life's journey has brought you to this point for a reason: to save your people."*

Mordecai's call to purpose works. It arouses Esther's desire to help and ability to be strong. She replies assuredly, and tells Mordecai to gather other Jews and fast for her. For in three days, she will enter the king's presence and deal with whatever consequences may come. Even if that means death.

This is a terribly important scene. One in which the entire story of Esther depends. If she had chosen differently, we could only imagine the consequences, and how the direction of God's people may have changed from that day forward.
But the good news is that we don't have to imagine, because Esther chose to be brave. She was able to do so, in large part, due to Mordecai's words. And his advice is as relevant today as it was back then.

Is there something you are scared to do? Or something you have put off doing? Not just for days, but for years? Is there a calling on your life that you have ignored, or convinced yourself that, even though you feel the desire to pursue it, it's just not what God has for you?

The truth is you're not alone. I have those things. We all do. The reason they stay undone and unpursued is not because we are bad or lazy people.

Yesterday we talked about how fear can stop us. It can become a roadblock in our paths to God's calling. But fear is just one roadblock. There are countless others like self-doubt, need, pain, greed, and many more. So if there are all these obstacles in the way, how will we ever get closer to what God may be calling us to?

The answer is in what Mordecai said. Mordecai helped Esther overcome her fear by calling out her purpose. Purpose is what turns obstacles into opportunities. When we have expended every ounce of our energy and hope, purpose is what comes in and refuels our tanks. Where Esther saw fear and the possibility of pain, Mordecai saw opportunity. Esther was there for a reason. It was that belief, that deep-seated emotion that she mattered in God's plan, which enabled her to accept the risk.

You may feel like you do not know your purpose, so let me tell you something I have found over and over again in Scripture. Purpose is discovered, one overcome obstacle at a time. The way we accomplish God's call on our lives is by approaching each difficulty and handling it in such a way that exults godly character, and displays trust in Him.
That is the reason we can never see our entire path or purpose all at once. Our purpose is revealed, and our path constructed, one obstacle at a time.

Takeaway: God's purpose for us is discovered by overcoming one obstacle at a time.

Prayer: You are a good, good Father. You know exactly how and why I was created. Help me honor You with each step I take towards the calling You have given me.

Esther's Strategy

Day 12

Esther 5:1-8

The time has come for Esther to enter the king's presence. She dons her royal robes and enters the throne room confidently. Xerxes reacts better than even she could have hoped. He is elated to see her and promises to grant her request, even up to half the kingdom!

The phrase *"up to half the kingdom"* was likely a contemporary expression, like we would say "you'll never believe this" when in fact, the listener probably will. However, Xerxes words do relate to his tendency to do everything in excess.[xi] Esther could have laid out her request then and there, but she goes about it in a much more strategic way.

Esther invites Xerxes and Haman to a banquet, where she will reveal her request. This strategy would not have been uncommon. Many "petitions and negotiations" were usually saved for after banquets and meals since both parties were likely to be more giving.[xii]

The narrator quickly speeds us along to the end of Esther's banquet. Will she make her request? How will the king react? What will happen to Haman? Unfortunately, we are made to wait a little longer. Esther uses her request to bring her two guests to a second banquet on the following day. At first glance, it appears as though Esther has chickened out. She couldn't bring herself to reveal the real issue, and so she has saved herself, at least for the moment, by delaying it.

In reality, Esther knows exactly what she is doing. "Esther is shrewdly and subtly pursuing a well-designed plan."[xiii] By postponing the reveal she has moved her two guests right to where she needs them. Xerxes will be both grateful and curious enough that he really will grant her any request. Haman will be so filled with pride because of the private invitations that he will be completely defenseless. Now, with her entire gameboard setup, we will see if her plan succeeds.

Strategy plays an important role in the story of Esther. It was Mordecai strategy which got Esther into the palace as queen. Esther's strategy helps change the fate of her people. Strategy also plays an important role elsewhere in Scripture. Matthew 10:16b tells us, *"Therefore be as shrewd as snakes."* Jesus tells his disciples this after giving them very specific instructions about who they should preach to and what towns they should go to.

I say all this because strategy seems to have gotten a bad rap in many Christian's minds. We hear verses like Proverbs 19:21, *"Many are the plans in a person's heart, but it is the LORD's purpose that prevails,"* and take it to mean that we shouldn't even bother making a plan. If I make a plan for my life, is that going against God's will or showing that I do not trust Him? Not at all.

Living our life with a plan shows that we have intent. Trying to live out the purpose God has called us to, without developing a strategy to do so, is irresponsible. Dave Ramsey, the creator of Financial Peace University, teaches us that it's impossible to honor God with your money without having a budget. Why? Because a budget gives our money strategy, and unless we make tithing and giving a part of our financial strategy – they just won't get done.

In the same way, if you feel you are called to serve in a particular ministry but never strategize about how you are going to fit it into your week, how likely is it that you are actually going to follow through? If you are in charge of putting together a missions trip for your church, how will it ever take place unless much strategy and thought goes into its preparation?

If purpose is the what that will drive our lives and relationships with God to greater heights, then strategy is the how. So where do we go from here? I do not know all the ins and outs of crafting a God-honoring strategy, but I do know where to start. The same place Esther did.

Before the banquets and before facing the king, Esther did the one thing every Christian's strategy requires: she prayed. There is no such thing as a God-honoring strategy that has not been grounded in prayer. Prayer binds our feet to solid ground as we dare to reach for Heaven's stars.

Takeaway: Pursuing our purpose requires strategy and strategy comes through prayer.

Prayer: Almighty God, there is nothing outside of Your control or that You do not understand. Grow in me a desire to pray, and a shrewdness for strategic living.

David Ramos

Our Happy Hearts

Day 13
Esther 5:9-14

As Esther's private banquet ends, Haman leaves feeling as though he is on top of the world. Here he was, having private meals with the king and queen. But that feeling was soon deflated as he walked by Mordecai.

Mordecai did not do anything disrespectful. The problem was, in fact, that Mordecai did nothing at all. He did not acknowledge Haman's presence, and Haman took it as disrespect. Angry and bothered he heads home to rant to his wife, named Zeresh. We don't learn much about her, but from the short bit of conversation it sounds as if she isn't too different from her husband.

As a remedy for Mordecai's disrespect, Zeresh urges her husband to build a wooden pole that is over 70 feet high and impale Mordecai on it. There is only one reason for it to be built so large. Haman will get more pleasure out of the masses seeing Mordecai suffer than he would making the man suffer in private.

Haman is thrilled by the idea and has it built that very day. Little does he know who will actually be on that pole tomorrow.

Haman's pride overwhelms this scene. It's clear where his priorities lie, mainly with himself. However, there is one phrase in particular we can learn from.

Verses 11 and 12 record Haman talking about everything he has: wealth, descendants, honor, and power. Then, in verse 13, he continues, *"But all this gives me no satisfaction."* How can this be? On paper, he is what we would call successful. Haman has a large family, a full bank account, and an important job that he appears to enjoy very much. Yet, the one thing that is keeping him from being happy is a stubborn old man named Mordecai.

If you want to truly know a person, find out what makes them happy and unhappy. That will reveal where their heart truly lies.

Haman was not a family man, a power grabber, or even greedy. These were all symptoms of the deeper problem: his uncontrollable pride. Mordecai could have stolen from Haman or even accidentally killed one of his sons – and neither of these actions would have made Haman as angry as showing him disrespect.

If we take the focus off Haman for a moment and move it on to ourselves, we can ask the same difficult questions. What is it that really makes me happy? What, more than anything, makes me unhappy or angry? There are no right or wrong answers here, only truth. We may find that we don't like the answers we give, and that is okay. Before we can become who God has called us to be, we must acknowledge who we currently are.

Takeaway: Our true priorities are revealed by what makes us happy and unhappy.

Prayer: Dear Lord, I surrender my heart and wants to You. As I learn to want the things You want, and hate the things You hate, I will live more like Jesus.

David Ramos

God of The Small

Day 14

Esther 6:1-5

Do you believe in coincidences? I used to. Sometimes, I think I still do. But when it comes to Scripture, you would be hard-pressed to find anything that would support the idea that true coincidences exist.

The dictionary defines coincidences as "a remarkable concurrence of events or circumstances without apparent causal connection."[xiv] Simply put, a coincidence is when things happen in a very unlikely way without anyone having made them happen that way. We also use the words "serendipity, chance, or happenstance" to describe these events.

When we come to the sixth chapter of Esther, we are faced with one of the most extraordinary series of coincidences one could ever imagine. The king cannot sleep and begins to read the precise section of the exact book that will save the life of his servant Mordecai, who is in risk of being killed by the very man arriving at that moment. I wonder if there are even numbers small enough to explain the likelihood of this scene progressing as it did!

Author John Piper summarizes what this scene should lead us to believe, "If there is a God in heaven, there is no such thing as a mere coincidence, not even in the smallest affairs of life."[xv] An all-powerful, all-wise, deeply involved God cannot exist alongside happenstance. He is guiding and crafting the world as He sees fit. He determines the path of world history even as He leads you to read the exact verse you need to hear on a difficult day. There is no limit to His reach, and there is no subject in His universe too small that He should not give it His full attention.

The entire book of Esther calls for us to see God's hand, even when He is silent. Sometimes God will break into our stories with miracles and unexplainable events. Other times He will simply move the pieces where they need to be, and whisper to you the words you need to say just as you are speaking them.

There are no coincidences because our great God never neglects the small.

Takeaway: Because God is in control, there are no coincidences.

Prayer: Lord, You are in control of the big and the small, the mighty and weak. Help me see Your hand in every coincidence.

Character And Influence

Day 15
Esther 6:6-14

Haman enters the king's presence at the best possible time for Mordecai, and the worst possible moment for himself.

The king asks how he should honor a loyal servant. Haman, blinded by pride, believes the king is referring to him. So he suggests an excessive, ego-boosting parade through the city. What comes next is deeply satisfying for every reader rooting for Mordecai.

There are a handful of moments in Scripture that I wish I could have been present at. Such as when David conquered Goliath or when Moses led his people to freedom. This moment is one I would loved to have seen: when Haman realizes that he is not, in fact, the one being honored. Instead, it is his sworn enemy. Not only will he not succeed in killing the man, he will be the one leading and praising Mordecai throughout the city! God's sense of justice is truly sweet.

After the festivities are over, we see Mordecai and Haman go their separate ways. Haman is humiliated. He runs home, distraught, and gets no help from his family. When they hear what has happened, they tell Haman that he will *"surely come to ruin."* Clearly, they are not the most well-functioning family.

Although the attention in this chapter is mainly focused on Haman, I don't want us to miss Mordecai's actions. In verse 12 it says, *"Mordecai returned to the king's gate."* It's a short, insignificant sentence. But it speaks volumes to Mordecai's character. This was Mordecai's chance. He could have belittled Haman, laughed at him, or really milked the situation for his benefit. Yet, we don't hear any such thing. Throughout the entire scene, not a single word from Mordecai is recorded, leading us to believe that he was silent. He did not seize the opportunity to harass Haman at his lowest point. Mordecai simply accepted the honor and, when it was over, went straight back to work.

Even though much of the book of Esther is not directly about her, it is about the events and people which influenced her. By now, Esther had been in the royal court for years. She saw loyalty and betrayal. She was beginning to understand what it took to rise in government; how to play the politics, and yet maintain strong alliances. But I believe more than any other influence, it was Mordecai who most shaped Esther's character. The humility and self-sacrifice we see in Esther can trace their roots back to Mordecai.

Often, our greatest influences do not bother to make themselves great. I know personally, two of my greatest influences have both been janitors. The way they worked and the way they served still pushes me to be a better Christian to this day. They embodied Galatians 6:9, "*Let us not become weary in doing good.*"

Take a moment today to remember who has influenced your life for the better. Who did God bring into your path that had a profound impact? What can you do today to show them your gratitude?

Takeaway: Remembering our influences can remind us of the path we want to be on.

Prayer: Thank You God for bringing amazing, humble, and honorable people into my lives. I want to both honor their example, and also become an example as You continue to mold me to your likeness.

Leading Well

Day 16
Esther 7:1-10

The moment we have been waiting for has arrived. Esther, the king, and Haman have all arrived for the second and final banquet. Curiosity has to be eating away at Xerxes and he wastes no time asking Esther, once again, what it is she wants.

Esther crafts a respectful, yet manipulative, reply. She does not rush in and blame Haman. Instead, she builds up the king's emotional response. Someone is out to get her and her people, someone who has been working right underneath the king's nose. We can imagine the scene: Esther's words growing louder and breaking as she holds back tears. Xerxes' face turning red with anger, and his voice yelling as he pleads for Esther to tell him who this man is.

It all comes to a head in verse 6 when Esther turns and points to Haman. The terror Haman must have felt. He had no warning, no inkling that he could possibly be in danger until the moment the queen uttered his name. His pride had blinded him. And it is his pride which expedites the coming judgment.

In an act of pure desperation, Haman begs the queen to spare his life. The king sees this and takes it as an assault against his queen. In the king's mind, Haman has sealed his fate. Before the reader can even process everything that has happened, a servant comes to tell the king about Haman's pole and without hesitation, Xerxes has Haman impaled on it.

Chapter 7 ends with the enemy of the Jews dead, but the threat to their lives still exists.

What I find interesting about this scene is that Xerxes takes no credit in making the edict against the Jews. Maybe he felt guilty, and that is why he ran out to the garden just as things were escalating. Maybe he felt no guilt at all.

The truth is, King Xerxes did not take responsibility for his part in Haman's plot. He blamed it all on his co-conspirator. That strategy might work for a king, but it will never work for a great leader.

It's impossible to lead well without taking responsibility. Xerxes showed us the example of what not to do. He was essentially a puppet, led around by his advisors. Then, if something went wrong, he could blame the advisor instead of accepting that he had been the one to make the decision. On the opposite end of the spectrum is Esther. Esther has made the welfare of the Jewish people her responsibility. She has identified herself with them and tied her fate to theirs.

Esther is the one history remembers for a reason, because she is the example we should follow.

Takeaway: You cannot lead if you do not take responsibility.

Prayer: Help me become a better leader in every area You have called me to Lord: family, church, work. I can hold responsibility because I know You are holding me.

David Ramos

The Ones God Chooses

Day 17
Esther 8:1-17

With Haman dead, Esther and Mordecai can now turn their attention to reversing the edict.

Chapter 8 begins with Xerxes gifting Haman's estate to Esther. We can guess that this gift was the king's way of saying sorry. But an apology is not what the Jewish people need most. Esther continues to plead before the king, asking him to revoke the previous edict.

He cannot. Instead, he does the only thing we have seen him capable of: turn over responsibility to others. Xerxes gives his signet ring to Mordecai and tasks his servant and his queen with fixing the situation by making a new edict. We can be disappointed in the king once again for not standing up, but at least he has given power to the right people this time.

Mordecai and Esther get right to work and construct a new rule which will allow the Jewish people to protect themselves and attack their enemies. The message is sent throughout the kingdom, delivered by the king's fastest horses. Now, all we can do is wait and hope that their plan will work.

Chapter 8 ends with an interesting line. It says, *"And many people of other nationalities became Jews because fear of the Jews had seized them."* Could you have imagined that outcome? A few moments ago, to be a Jew was the most dangerous identity in the kingdom. Non-Jews avoided them, and we can believe that many Jewish people hid their heritage out of fear. But the tables have turned. To be Jewish was not shameful but desired. The same people who avoided the Jews out of fear of danger are now joining them for safety!

This is how God works. He takes the ones the world has abandoned and elevates them to be sought after. We are to be like children, to love the weak, and to remember the lonely. Why? Because these are the ones God has his eye on. These ones God stays close to.

If you are reading this, chances are you have been on the receiving end of loss or abandonment in your own life. How can I know that? Because no person gets through this life unscathed; God's children most of all. However, let this be an encouragement to you. God wants to take your trouble and redeem it. He wants to take your pain and transform it into an opportunity.

It was the part of Esther's story that she hid, which God used for a mighty purpose. You were chosen for a reason; and more often than not, that reason has to do with God bringing good into the world out of the things we hide.

Takeaway: God uses every part of our story for His glory.

Prayer: Father, it's hard for me to imagine how You can use all of me. But I will trust You.

David Ramos

Redeeming Treasures

Day 18

Esther 9:1-19

This scene is not, and should not, be an easy section of Scripture to read. Both Haman's and Esther's edicts have gone out into the world, and the day has come for the Jews to defend themselves against their enemies.

The text tells us that the Jewish people assembled, probably to make their defense stronger, and that the leaders of each city and town sided with the Jews and fought on their side. What came next was undisputed victory for the Jews. They killed at least 500 of their enemies, along with the remaining members of Haman's family.

On top of all this, the king offers Esther one more request. She asks if the day could be extended so that even more of their enemies could be wiped out. The request is granted and at least 300 more people are killed during the extra day.

It's a bloodbath. I always come to this portion of the text with mixed feelings. On the one hand, we can celebrate because the Jewish people have succeeded. They were not only saved, but they prevailed over the enemies in a huge way. Yet on the other hand, what we are seeing is essentially "Haman's plan in reverse."[xvi]

Do you know that scene in movies where the hero has the chance to kill the main enemy, but another character convinces them not to or else "you'll be just as bad as they are?" That is what sticks in my mind as I read this passage.

These difficult parts have important lessons to teach us about how we should interact with the Bible. I want to share two of them below.

The first is one you may have heard before: the difference between descriptive and prescriptive. The entire Bible can be broken down into two very simple categories. Descriptive means the text is telling us about something. It is merely a catalog of events and stories. Those stories may have lessons to offer about God, life, and other topics. But that is a secondary purpose. The second type is prescriptive which means the text is meant to tell us why or how we should do something. The most notable examples of this would be Jesus' sermons or Paul's letters. Those parts of the Bible are packed with applicable advice that Christians should put into use immediately.

There is not a strict line between these two categories. Many descriptive stories in the Bible have prescriptive elements, and vice versa. But it's an important question to ask the text, especially when you come to a passage like this one: is this passage telling me about something that happened, or telling me how I should act?

I believe this violent scene is largely descriptive. There are lessons we may be able to take about self-defense, or how God judges the enemies of his people. There is even a lesson about learning from history, as I will explain below. However, the ending of Esther (both chapters 9 and 10) are meant to tell a story, not a way of acting.

The second big lesson I want to share is a reminder that all of Scripture is connected. Do you remember earlier when I explained Haman and Mordecai's backgrounds? As a quick recap, Mordecai could trace his lineage back to King Saul and Haman could trace his back to King Agag.

There's a phrase that pops up 3 times in this passage: *"but they did not lay their hands on the plunder."* A curious reader might think that this is just a phrase extolling the Jews for not being greedy. When in fact, it's a call to remember something that happened in 1 Samuel 15.

Saul lost his favor with God, and ultimately his kingship, because he took the plunder after he defeated Agag. Even after God had told him specifically not to. Chapter 9 of Esther acts as a redemption story for Saul's mistake. They did what Saul refused to do: defeat their enemy, but leave the enemy's plunder untouched. This tie with another Biblical story sheds a completely different light upon the scene.

All this is to say, I wish for you to become close readers of Scripture. God's grace is sometimes hidden in the details. And when you are looking for an answer to your prayer or a sign of guidance for your life, it's often those tiny treasures which can dramatically change our lives.

Takeaway: When we plant ourselves in difficult parts of Scripture, we will reap beautiful treasures.

Prayer: Almighty God, Your Word is a gift – one I am learning how to use better each and every day. Guide me towards your truths, especially the ones which require some digging.

David Ramos

His Final Word

Day 19
Esther 9:20-32

As we near the end of Esther's story, the book concludes in a similar way to how it began, with a party.

The two days of bloodshed turn into a celebration for the Jewish people. They have triumphed against all odds, and now those two dates will be remembered through celebration. It's important to note that the reason they are celebrating is not to wipe away the pain of what had happened.[xvii] Rather, they institute the holiday as an opportunity for remembrance. The holiday will remind them of the danger they faced, and how God delivered them (partly through the actions they chose to take).

Verse 26 tells us the festival was named Purim after the word pur. It is the name of the lot (a stone with symbols on it) that Haman cast when the date for his evil plan was first decided. The festival is made official by Queen Esther and Chapter 9 ends with an assurance that this holiday will continue down through every generation.

Esther is a difficult story to study because it is many stories intertwined into one. We talked about how part of Esther is a comedy – the story is progressed through reversals and unexpected events. Esther also has historical elements. The writer wants to pull us into the Persian world, and help us understand what the Jews were truly up against. Finally, the book of Esther is also an etiology for the festival of Purim. An etiology is simply an origin story, or a retelling of how something came to be. The most popular etiology is Noah and the ark. One of the purposes of that story is to tell us how rainbows were made.

We are a hodge-podge of stories as well. Our lives are a beautiful mess of events, trials, successes, and reversals. As we love and work and grow, our stories become intertwined with others. Where we go to school, who we marry, where we work – these all impact how we see the world and, ultimately, how the world will see us.

When I read this chapter, in all its layered complexity, and think about what the festival must have meant to the Jewish people, I am hit with a single phrase: God always has the final word. The mess of that dangerous situation, much like the mess of our lives, is never so chaotic that it is out of God's control.

In the book of Esther, we never see God's hand supernaturally appear. We don't have the name of God, or even the word "God" uttered once throughout the entire book. And yet, He is intimately at work. God is present in a secular world. Although He may not speak where the people do not know His name, or acknowledge His power, He is there. He is the God of all creation with authority over every being. Both those who love Him and those who do not. And we are fully, desperately His.

Takeaway: God is in control and has the final word.

Prayer: Father, help me know You are near. You are my God and I trust my messy life and this messy world into Your hands.

Chosen

The final chapter of Esther closes with a hopeful outlook for the Jewish people.

Once again, readers are reminded of the power and size of the Persian empire. Only now, the purpose is not to introduce us into a world of excess, but to show us how far Mordecai has come. Because of his loyal service to both the king and his people, Mordecai has been elevated to *second in rank to King Xerxes.* In the span of a few chapters, we have seen God raise two of His people to some of the highest offices in all the land.

Esther, a Jewish orphan who was raised by her kind cousin, is now the queen of one of history's greatest empires. Mordecai, a humble servant who gave of himself to help others whenever possible, is now able to dramatically influence the world for good.

This final chapter is meant to offer us hope. We too, are foreigners in a strange land. The Christian life can be a difficult one as we traverse the Earth, fulfilling God's call, and look forward to the day He calls us home. But if we think that this life is meant to be spent primarily thinking about the next, we are missing out on something so incredibly beautiful.

The story of Esther and Mordecai shows us that God has a purpose for putting us in this world. We were created to live lives of profound impact, to reshape history, and to fill this Earth with good works so that others may benefit and *"glorify [our] Father in heaven."*[xviii]

I pray that the story of Esther will impress upon you your own chosenness. There is a reason you are a here, a reason you have felt God's call upon your life, and a reason you have come to this very page.

May you seek God with the boldness of Esther, the wisdom of Mordecai, and the belief that, truly, you were made for such a time as this.

Takeaway: I have been chosen by God for great works, for His glory.

Prayer: Thank You Lord for choosing me. I do not know the adventure You have for me, but I know that You chose me for a reason.

Continuing the Journey

Thank you for reading *Chosen with Esther*. I hope the experience was encouraging and that you've learned just a little bit more about one of the most selfless characters in the Old Testament.

Now that you've started to learn some Old Testament truths, here are two steps you can take to continue your journey.

First, sign up for my newsletter at RamosAuthor.com. There you'll receive a monthly email that contains exclusive insights, book discounts, and the free gift *Dreaming with Joseph*.

Second, please take a minute to write a short review for *Chosen with Esther* on Amazon. These reviews help me write better, more effective books so I would deeply appreciate your support!

The one lesson from Esther's life that I will never forget is this: God wants to use all of your story for His glory. Esther was thrust into a position of power she never asked for, while hiding a background she had no reason to be ashamed of. God used Esther mightily, not in spite of who she was, but because she was the exact person needed for that moment in history. I pray you will realize you are just as important, in your own unique way, as Esther was.

I hope you will take the challenge and live a life characterized by a trust in God's plan. It will be difficult, but never forget that you were chosen!

David Ramos

About the Author

David Ramos is an author and teacher passionate about communicating the life-changing truths found in the Old Testament. He has a degree in Classical and Medieval Studies and is currently finishing a Master's in Religion (Biblical Studies) at Ashland Theological Seminary. When he's not writing you can usually find David chasing down the newest food truck or helping his fiancé Breahna plan their wedding (2016).

David and his library currently reside in Cleveland, Ohio.

Visit his website at ramosauthor.com or on Facebook.com/DavidRamosAuthor.

More Books by David Ramos

The Bible Habit: 7 Strategies on How to Study the Bible

Daring with Ruth: 18 Devotionals to Ignite Your Courage, Transform Your Hope, and Reveal God's True Character

Crowned with David: 40 Devotionals to Inspire Your Life, Fuel Your Trust, and Help You Succeed in God's Way

Enduring with Job: 30 Devotionals to Give You Hope, Stir Your Faith, and Find God's Power in Your Pain

Climbing with Abraham: 30 Devotionals to Help You Grow Your Faith, Build Your Life, and Discover God's Calling

Escaping with Jacob: 30 Devotionals to Help You Find Your Identity, Forgive Your Past, and Walk in Your Purpose

The God with a Plan

The Shadow of Gethsemane: An Easter Poem

Further Reading on Esther

Esther Scroll: The Story of the Story by David J. A. Clines

Esther: A Woman of Strength and Dignity by Charles R. Swindoll

Esther: It's Tough Being a Woman by Beth Moore

Esther by John Piper

Takeaway List

1. Excess, in any area of life, will eventually lead to pain.

2. As we observe what is happening in our lives, it's important that we also learn to ask the why and how behind it.

3. What we allow ourselves to listen to and believe, will profoundly shape our lives.

4. There are no coincidences, only designed opportunities.

5. Nothing in this life can subtract from the value God has given me.

6. We can neither earn God's grace, nor imagine where it will take us.

7. God's authority should be the most important authority in our lives.

8. Ignoring God can lead to blindness. Blindness

can lead us down paths we never thought we would go. But God's grace always offers us a way back to Him.

9. Our hope in God is fueled by our knowledge of His character.

10. Your fear never has to be the end of the road.

11. God's purpose for us is discovered by overcoming one obstacle at a time.

12. Pursuing our purpose requires strategy and strategy comes through prayer.

13. Our true priorities are revealed by what makes us happy and unhappy.

14. Because God is in control, there are no coincidences.

15. Remembering our influences can remind us of the path we want to be on.

16. You cannot lead if you do not take responsibility.

17. God uses every part of our story for His glory.

18. When we plant ourselves in difficult parts of Scripture, we will reap beautiful treasures.

19. God is in control and has the final word.

20. I have been chosen by God for great works, for His glory.

[i] Peter R. Barkworth, "The Organization of Xerxes' Army"http://www.azargoshnasp.net/300/xerxesorganizationarmy.pdf

[ii] Frederic W. Bush, *Ruth, Esther* from *Word Biblical Commentary* (Nelson Reference and Electronic, 1996), 350-351.

[iii] Ibid., 353.

[iv] Adele Berlin, *Esther* from *The JPS Bible Commentary* (Philadelphia: The Jewish Publication Society, 2001), xvi-xxii. This section address Esther's comedic elements in greater depth.

[v] Ibid., 26.

[vi] Bush, 374.

[vii] Ibid., 384.

[viii] Ibid., 388.

[ix] Ibid., 393.

[x] http://www.dictionary.com/browse/fear

[xi] Bush, 406.

[xii] Ibid., 404.

[xiii] Ibid., 407.

[xiv] https://www.google.com/webhp?sourceid=chrome-instant&ion=1&espv=2&ie=UTF-8#q=concidence

[xv] http://www.desiringgod.org/articles/isn-t-it-ironic

[xvi] Bush, 463.

[xvii] Ibid., 492.

[xviii] Matthew 5:16.

Made in the USA
Lexington, KY
10 June 2017